A Ride through Heaven's Ranch

BY KODY D. KIND

DORRANCE PUBLISHING CO
EST. 1920
PITTSBURGH, PENNSYLVANIA 15238

Dorrance Publishing Co
585 Alpha Drive
Suite 103
Pittsburgh, PA 15238
Visit our website at *www.dorrancebookstore.com*

ISBN: 979-8-88925-072-2
eISBN: 979-8-88925-572-7

A Ride through Heaven's Ranch

Foot's Stream

Lonesome, music trickles into my heart. The plummeting triumphs of moving on crash across the rocks. This stream brings life to all living creatures. The serendipity of the stream brings hope to a lonesome soul. I sit and wonder while I ponder about the emptiness found in the world. The feeling of this stream's waterfall as it seems to never end. To want to fly only to cry and wishing to die. The doves of love never lands in the sands, it is only found through heart breaks. The emptiness of small abysses that surround this stream from high waters that left before a job was done. Leave tiny homes for those who dwell in cool nestling muck. A pretentious leap from a bullfrog surprises all that found shade in the water crest. The flat shells of limestone sliding down one another to reach a new home, and a new beginning. The green that sounds you seems so full and lush. As squirrels dance among the limbs trying to find a snack. The birds that can live above the clouds still choose to be here. To die before they can cry is the reason they fly. I walk along this cattle rut that cohabitates with the changing stream. Chasing the views that lay beside it. I look upon limestone, as big as mountains, that protrude through the crust of earth as giants ready to reclaim their land. The grace they uphold as life has grown in every crevice of them, as though big teddy bears nurturing the life they hold. Crossing fences patched together like man. Whatever could be scavenged now lays in hopes of strung out wire crippled by the rust that entangles its destined decay. Stretching out where the water leaves flats without the protection of trees across a meadow. So golden with the fluent motion of a rising sea. It carries upon the flats, as hidden beds lay the sea to rest. Where deer have called home from night to night. The subtle mounds of calm badgers crease each terrace. Knowing not to intrude upon their land the journey continues. Carving the land with softening banks only finding few places for those who pass it to cross. For in places the raw power of this stream's life roars on, while in others it lay so calm, bleak, and stagnant. Every place along its shores are bound to a new glimpse of hope. To wonder as I ponder, finding that each moment holds new relevance in the shallow places in life. I crave the crusading leaves that hitchhike their way across barren ground, to a new home of wilting away to watch a new sun set. At the end of this stream lies a river. Once a strong divider where they went their separate ways now eroded down to a shared marking of reliance. Where the stream once moved on now, it falls into bigger and better that swallows up its grace in a dwindling sense of exhaustion. To some it seems only natural, to others it is a sense of giving up on the stream's part. Leaving those downstream to fend for themselves. To die before it can fly is the reason it cries.

The Ride into Heaven's Ranch

As the morning is still young, long before the sun rises in the east, bringing crystals upon the land from the frost that lay still asleep. Hearing the coffee boil amongst crackling embers of hedge. As feet slide onto the frost bitten floor, skin cripples as the chill of the night has not yet left the room. Eyes are still glazed over from sleep, struggling to close them again. Breathing in air so clean and crisp that the throat suffers a dry and burning pain. Arms coil around the body like snakes squeezing every ounce of life out, in order to gain a second of warmth. The subtle blissfulness of a breeze whispers sweet joys. Listening, as the gate I walk through each day no longer stands broken and abused, but rather homely, as it squeaks open and slams shut. My eyes only understand what is within reach as I walk drearily toward the barn. I look down at hands that show more stories than you or I could tell. Each scar, callus, rope burn, and lost fingernail shows the story of what the owner has already forgotten.

As I look upon my hallowed barn, the faint sight of stained red streaks of shed blood show. The skeleton shows through where its flesh has been ripped away. By the pain brought upon it through the years it has endured. Where eyes of glass used to see clearly, now they are fogged over for the world to see. Once a refuge from the world, now short of the tin hairs left on its head. The bellows of vibrations shake the ground as mothers search for their young. A soft caressing breath is exhaled with steam. An animal I have only known as a friend and partner through my years calls upon me from his stall. I watch as the fading smoke vaporizes into the arising sun. The horse, my coffee, and smoke are all gone without a trace as the day prolongs.

The shackles I call spurs bring me home without allowing me to leave. They ring through the day at every hitch I come upon. My frails swirl, whirling with the spirit's breath as my chaps crash like waves upon me. The subtle rubbing of leather as a saddle is cinched tight reminds me of my yesterday. The calmness of an aching body riding out into the world he has only ever known as home. The sapphire begins upon the hills as thundering hooves chase it to rise first. The silent air teaches the trees that their solitude can still be enjoyed. Royalty of the Romans cover the earth's floor as flowers of purple so intimately gather upon the prairie. The chance of seeing the prairie's leopards this time of year excite the land as new fawns dance upon dirt in a ballet of learning that strikes their feet. Green, still far and few between, seem immersed upon the Kansas fields as a winter crop shows its growth through the harshness of winter. Where once unsettled lands so clear under the velvet of powdered snow now lay varnished and scared as man's hand has slid upon them. While humanity curses the land, the treasures left behind are that of poetry. As the fallen hay of fall rests upon the plains, it is the true frosting of nature, causing even me to be famished by such a large delicious sight.

As I crest the river valley, to what a sight I behold as the ice is shown true and pure, similar to one's young, naive heart. It is untouched and so beautiful as the world is reflected upon it. Yet, stampeded upon by one's own negligence shows how fragile the heart can be when broken too soon. It is meant to flow on never knowing the next bend or what it holds with issue. It is powerful and strong in moments, and shallow and weak in times of crossings. The birds bring upon songs of friends that have floated- in and out of life causing one to smile upon their song as they disappear into the depths of a vast ocean of sky. The prairie is so bare, yet a lone tree will stand in the sight of a picture for someone's album. Years of solitude, stories, scars, and life has come around this tree. Now nothing more than shade, pictures, and firewood will ever become of it. A sense of company evokes a man's natural curiosity as the trust he bears over that land and animals he claims as his own. The random sense of heaven can be heard along thrusting grasses. The sound of spring frogs croaking under false hope of summer. The quiet trickles of a stream that is only let down to cause an eruption. Once so peaceful, now a glisten of hope. The calming crackles of trees too tall for survival soon to fall before autumn. Their leaves weigh so little, yet gather among the branches, pulling the tree's life away as the wind cradles it to the floor. The mystic rumbles of thunder in a faraway land bring hope to those downstream. The calming essence of euphoria eases its way into a man's heart as a herd of healthy prime angus stand alone, chewing cud of yesterday's triumph. Those souls that could not hang onto their original homes drift along the crust of the earth searching for wherever the wind takes them.

The essence of family ties arise among the corrals that have been branded and bruised upon their fence posts, barely placed together through generations of repairs. The ride home after the sun has graced the earth, washing away the crystals of night's frost, warms the body far beyond that which lay still on the plains. It shows all the hidden evils merely passable in the dark. The home of badgers that lay under a horse's feet show the trust of health amongst one's relationship. The hills rise and vanish upon the horizons of the eye, simply catching beautiful glimpses of what is yet to be discovered. The fence that corrals the life he has worked so long to build seems to reflect his own soul. The post once strong from being cut and beaten now lay hopeless. Thinking they know where they stand, only for little holes to slowly be punched through them as each invading year sets upon new tales of nature. The wires show how the purpose of a man is learned through constant action. They drag closer and closer to the ground each year as they stretch from cattle grazing, to the snow and moon that lay upon them year after year. They know that like the soul, its only purpose, through scarred posts and dragging wire, is to keep it all in and is worth a lifetime of suffering.

Devastation of nature causes the broken tree to lay in a path, while unsettling upon its discovery, the jagged edges of age rings cut through the scenery as unnatural. The broken bits of homes, and habitats sectioned off as though the animals claimed their mortgage. Devastation, nonetheless, holds its own purpose through nature even as the reasons why are unexplained. The evils of nature will pursue a man to expose the faults of thy own devastation. From the thrills of a hired hand free as the clouds to soar, but come alone, the hopes of a working man who lives by schedule in a dire need of lost schedules. The hate developed through years of temptation. The anger brewed upon a man from those in his life that only seem to stand their ground, never understanding the feelings of nature, derived more than what humanity ever could for him. The scars that have cut so deeply through him are still filled with the pain and knowledge of past corruption. The desperation that once drew a trembling eagerness to his face now rests behind dead eyes of sorrow. The years of abusive physical labor demand on the payments of pain. The skin stretched and burned to a sagging leather that rests upon his bones. To be healed, heard, loved, taught, compassionate, and at home among the natures is all that was ever wanted. Yet, the work must be done in order to keep nature a part of a man's world.

The way to keep with modern times upon land and beast is to throw thine own permanent mark upon it all as to claim that which cannot be claimed as a symbol. The brand that crests each signature, each cow, each horse, each barn, and home all rest in peace of blood under the brim of a young man's hat. The eyes of the man sharp as a hawk before a strike, prey as they cower like a rabbit, sad as the mare whose first foal just lay limp upon the ground. Tragic like the heifers first calf as the penetration of needles and tags scorn its body. The evils that must be done under brim and through the eyes of the man are only done in preservation of tomorrow. The lives gathered upon the land seem yet to know the devastation of man as the contemporary housing of the man with few brutalities strikes them from home. The man sees the beauty of the land and the depression of a heart with a suppressed mind hold. The ride home is never as blossoming as the ride out.

The true diminish from nature is the nature of humanity. So selfishly wrapped up in individuals that the larger scale view of those who tend to more than themselves know. We stand strong to our individual selves and scandalize those who stretch for others. We cause ourselves hell to appease those who only appease themselves thinking they have contributed to us. Pain comes from giving everything you love behind to help one person and watching as they try to take your help and realize they do not understand all you went through to allow this. The acts of a selfless man do nothing for him aside from doing God's word. Which is all he needs only to be heartbroken again and again in the littlest of moments. The only things that mean a lick of truth are the moments when his teeth chipped from gritting so hard as excitement and exhilaration filled his body while a punch was thrown or a bone was broken.

He enjoys the physical pains of the life he chose as they hurt so little compared to the hurt he holds in his heart. No matter who tries to help or no matter the circumstances, he is meant for nothing more than a thrill, memory, and mistakes. He knows the truth and accepts it, yet does not show it through his day-to-day life. The wisdom he knows comes from the whiskey he drowns in. He knows truths only through fulfillment not through false lies. He is encouraged by the red eye that leads him to heartbroken places as he feels he belongs. When he awakens he knows only regret. He knows shame, doubt, humility, and loss. The only truths are through the night before, and the Marlboro memory as the morning carries the smoke away. The truth, even with his love, is never what he needs. Nothing is ever catered to those with broken hearts. There is always a deception hiding in someone's eyes. He knows it, he has lived it, yet he hopes for heaven. His prayers seem heard, but he will not complain about the little things. The truth lies between the whiskey and smokes.

However, the angel dressed as the devil welcomes the nature of life. For not all humanity does is out of nature. The capsizing moment of one's own clothes wrapped sleekly around the body of tomorrow. The sigh of a heart as nature's partner stands amongst the home which nature allowed. As the sensations of fear, anger, bliss, joy, compassion, devastation, and beauty all acquired in nature rest upon the back porch as sapphire hair swirls over her shoulders. The soft worn flannel that caresses her, once shared your body. The fibers of condensed pressure squawk beneath her every step. The trails of life that once stretched like cattle ruts, streamed along hillsides like roads in Italy winding and never having a direction, now know where one must suffer for heaven's reach is there. Much like nature, daily life may lead to devastation of beauty. I know before the glimpse of heaven can be seen again, the chores of life must come first to be fruitful. The barn that sways closer to the ground each day shows the age upon which I have left upon my steed with the sway back of his shoulders. I know the miles, the trust, the bucks, the fights, the moments of not knowing that sits upon the sway back with experience of trust. The saddle that weighs more each day shows miles of bad judgment, bad judgment that lead to experience, and experience that lead to good judgment. The bosal that lays upon the snout of my bay would say the tenderness of neck rein is the only way to treat wisdom.

The equipment that lays upon the yard as I venture home shows the generations of neglect in a man as blood rust the decaying surface, the fluids restrained of hopes to run again, the subtle elegance of a picture strikes my mind again. The limestone steps which embrace this gypsy soul stay solid and true through the muck drug upon them. I sit and ponder all that nature holds. As I embrace the rocking chair of age and pain and the porch where many of life's judgments were made, the beer, the lies, and the smokes that have crusted the floor of this porch all lead to the moment I aspired to be in right now. As the screen door slams shut with a sigh of irritation, I hear the angel of this life bringing me nourishment from the day. As I look upon the trees, the streams, the prairie, the colors, the depressions, the devastations, the miracles, the magic, and listen to the sounds of the years of nature have all waited to bring me, I realized I have just rode into heaven.

Nature is the only truth to a man. The only place where alone with thoughts, wants, needs, and love are welcomed with no judgment, only rawness. Where all of heaven meets. Where the trees shade only a corner of the branding pen. Where confusion, hope, skill, trust, anger, luck, and passion all grow their meaning. It all happens with the swing of a rope. The buck of a three year old. The loop of a beginner next to a veteran, the brand sizzled into hides forever. Blood shed through notched ears and cuts. Medicines to save health for tomorrow. Anger and aggression thrown out as toughness hides the place of it, confusing it as confidence. The partnership that shares a trust of catching to save the day. The passion of spreading life and life's purpose to more than just a family. The way dirt turns to dust, the way fence posts stand stronger than ever, the way a fire's crackle serves for more than light or warmth. The way a hat settles more on today, than on what's next. The one time of year when heaven meets earth is during branding. Where everything you crave from life is there. Calmness, wildness, truth, anger, pain, joy, triumph, where all the work pays off. To see the balances of nature mean more than a philosophical definition. If nature could do anything for a man, I hope nature gives every man the chance of my heaven's branding day. Where the sweat and countless prayers all pay off through the work they have trained so hard for. Dreams are nature and it gives it to us each day. It is when a man discovers his nature that nature heals him.

Nature gives no breaks and shows us the worst of life. Even in those moments, we see beauty. Even as she brings the worst, she also shows us our best. When all is bright, green, and warm we cluster to her. Nature is the most beautiful balance that gives and takes life as she pleases. Even when heaven tears are shed, and even in heaven, do we become thankful for the work, the death, the life, the calluses, the steam, the land, the hope, the glory, the dreams, the everything. It will trip you up and build you new again. To see your first born calf, to feel your first daily catch, to feel when your foal dies, to watch the tag numbers grow, to watch the seasons come and go, to watch your first steps as a man be that in which nature wanted. To have all that is welcomed and to know that even in the dark, the stars show us the suns of yesterday will be there for our memories. To know the natures come full circle to give us what we need in humanity. We are nothing more than nature itself. It needs us and we need them. That is what makes life in nature a ride through heaven.

Through all the experiences one can have in nature they all hold a divine purpose. Whether you map the rivers that tie each section of land back to the bigger oceans or if you hide from society within it, you can search for lost people who lived and learned of the land long before us. To research plants, rocks, trees, birds, fish, or animals, each piece of nature's offerings heal us in ways we did not know we needed. It holds answers to fears or questions that we ponder. Each man derives his own meaning to what nature can bring even if it is trying to avoid nature entirely. Each person holds their own heaven as a part of their personal nature. For me, nature is all the feelings that flood my mind and body. It is a home that allows me to escape everything but myself. I can turn views, sounds, jobs, and pain into poetry. It is not that I wish to, but it is how I find the beauty through all of them and why I enjoy all of them knowing I immersed myself in isolation to a home where man's hand has not begun its decay. I can be where I am at any point in humanities' timeline and see the same view. I can prophesy that all of our rat races are meaningless in such a short span of life compared to the land. I can tell you that even as we destroy nature, it will live on long past humanity. Nature is more than a home, a friend, a therapist, a story, a study, or a habitual healing place. To me, nature is heaven and I get to ride through it as new suns erase my time clock. I am allowed to walk through the gardens and know each moment is but a blink in my story. I know the scars the land has left on me and the scars I have left on it. To understand nature is never the purpose, but rather to not understand,

and walk blindly into your nature and experience each piece, and to know that no nature besides that of the hurt, scared, and protective natures will attack you. Physically or mentally, it is all a process within the trust of the beholder. Nature will always be here for us to hide in and scribe. However, nature can only hold its subjective meanings to you.

As I wrap up this paper please take a moment to find your heaven and take a walk through it. Do not look for the bad things, but rather find yourself and experience yourself. Find the beauties of your own walk and discover your nature through nature. Whatever your desire of thrill seeking or leisure lazy, search for nothing. Chance it to the tops of the hill, cling to the slow moment, find the thrills of your own branding pen, and strive to understand that there is no understanding, but simply the momentary discoveries along the way. Nature is a blessing we all share. It will surprise you and it will comfort you. Treat the natures as it treats you and fall in love with your walk through heaven. It will be your only chance. I hope the natures give you the closer or filling heart that it has given me. Now I must go and return to my walk through heaven as I hear the bellowing mothers stirring and my bay saying it is time to chase a new sunrise over the horizon. So, I will bid thee goodbye, as my angel is waiting in the gateway, so we may ride through our heaven.

The Narrows

Oh if only the words a man portrays could depict beauty of the astonishing views that forsake him. There is a niche that hides at the end of a finger. Where heaven forgot to leave the earth. Here as though like a child lost in a magical world. It is a grueling trip in that you must stomp through swampy marshes of stagnant sewer filled cesspools. To climb constantly up and down washed out river bottoms, and over tree roots that protrude from earth's floor. The mosquitoes that swarm you are enough to drive anyone insane. You cut, climb, claw, and clammer your way into a dense darkness of forest. You trek for what seems like ages chasing deer trails through poison ivy patches. Right when you believe no man could go further. There is always a ray of light that never misses this place. It is a tiny piece of the land that is stretched out in a finger. The river barely touches the property, but outlines this hamlet. As if you walked through a door the lights turn on, and everything is as you dream. The grass lay so low, and thick. Nestled up to the trunks of the trees. Where rainbows bounce off the wings of all that inhibit the place. The bosom of the forest is covered in purity as the blooming white flowers scent the early summer air. Pristine royalty make this humble circular patch. Sycamore trees freshly peeled in the warmth of light. So prominent against the green garden. Young coons chase their mother in aspirations of the next meal. While the troublemakers play in the back of the line. They follow the leader along the ground, then up the tree and stand confident along thin little branches. The tiny shakes that allow their fur to flow like wheat before harvest. They pass over the river without a drop, from limb to limb. The waters flow so smooth over the rapids hardly making a trickling noise. The shallows clear to the bottom as the rolling rocks sunk beneath rivers touch. Carp scramble in a tantrum trying to get further upstream. Gar shimmer with dotted tails as they gasp for air leaving behind endless circles to wave out to the banks. Beneath the sycamores lays a small shell rock bank. Where three foot flats make for a relaxing seat. Few clouds ever seem to float over this haven. Songs seem to flow into a man's mind when he sits in a place like this. No normalcies can reach him. The garden is what I call this place. It is a place where a man can escape. The creek makes a horse shoe and connects back into itself. Where it meets back up with itself, there is a small four foot waterfall where dirt and gravel banks have caved under pressure. Empty muscle shells left behind like dinner plates that lay along the shores from those who mingle in the moonlight. Knowing the journey back also a guidance in wanting a man to stay longer. Knowing the discovery of this place was a lost mistake. Now it is the only place I wish to collect my thoughts. The brand that marks all under my name now lays upon a sycamore for the world to see. It felt wrong after doing so, but the thought of the forest welcoming me back each time without dismay. Allows me to understand how special this grove feels knowing someone has wondered upon it and taken refuge. No destruction, only dedication to the health and beauty of life from the both of them. This place is the divider of worlds. It strips away all the other lives you live and have lived. Nothing more than alone man may enter to be saves, and nothing may be packed in through the journey here. So, here I sit along the edge of this hamlet knowing the trail back. Taking a look around for a memory until my next visit. The birds banter the sky with blues, orange, yellow, black, and the profound reds that cardinals claim as their own. The songs leave the echoes bouncing from each wall that resides this garden. The calming waters where fish seem to say hello without fear of hurt. Simply curiosity crossing all the animals that seem to find man in such a lost place. The trees slap their leaves together to wave one last time as I exit the garden and wonder back into grim darkness, where the stench of neglect has washed in and rested. The bugs that live in this world the blood suckers of annoyance. Only to reside back in another world where another heaven exist with all the other lives lived. The tiny hamlet

I can hide from is a constant home in my heart knowing I can be the only one to know its place. The place that welcomes only me. Where no destruction may come to it.

13

Lessons from Above

Lessons of Life show themselves with nothing more than to search for them. Man's world will deteriorate your meaning for life. If you fall to corruption of the paper that we share as currency takes over. Leaving many to return to nature in hopes that in the bareness of isolation, an answer can be found to help their tired souls. Lessons are taught as we skim the grounds of aloneness. Trees teach the solitude that time has. To stay in one place is scary to think about. Only to have lived so long only to see the same view. The trees say otherwise as they dance like children amongst themselves, to enjoy the harshness of reaching for 3the sun each day. They are allowed to see the prospering life that happens below them. The breath of new life, the end of one at the jaws of others, and the love that flourishes between the wildlife each year. The leaves of this tree are teaching us about love. They grow up together side by side. Choosing one another as the seasons of life go on. They partner up and fall for each other and crash upon earth's floor. They keep the spark of love alive, even after their time of growing old. Still playing tag in the aggressive autumn winds. Finally, they rest and fade away together welcoming new life under them. Rivers that allow all the trash of the world to fall into their flow, teach us the path of life. Where the turns can never be seen. The log jams that slow us down and clog us up. We can see that we can push by them. Knowing that all of our journey leads us to, is the next life that leads to bigger pools of water. The sands that lay on the hills show us adolescence in hope. So shifty and free clinging to whatever we stick to. Untouched like a blanket of caramel smooth, unscathed, unscared, and full of potential. Yet, stomped upon it is unsettled and thrown into the air. Pieces of itself sent off never to be a part of the hill again. It softens the world, yet stomped on it is lost forever. The weakness shown by the death in youth. No matter the strength, the tears shed as a mother loses her first born. The cries of a doe as a fawn falls from the banks, the bellows of cattle bawling for their children as they are hauled away, the broken leg of a foal whose first hours of life spent surrounded by coyotes. The last generation of bald eagles screeching as it falls from its nest. Pride shown through the pack. Pride and community shown through the cubbies of quail that have faced every danger, yet sing through the hollers as day breaks. The strength of pride shown through the dead coyote laid to waste by a mother who demanded no as an answer. The pride of wood ducks as they repeat their soft whistles through the valleys from escaping hunters, predators, and weather. The moods taught through the seasons of life. As green, new, and full of life is all that can be blessed and appreciated. Through heat waves that bring us close to water, the anger we hold is only being cooled by the things we hold, as neutral ground for all we hold close. The reds of autumn that show us later years as new life now on its own. The white blankets that hide all the bad under the purity of snow. We know there are moments where life is green and we know the joys of all the new we get to experience. The anger we feel as the world seems too much only having a few puddles of joy that bring us to fall. Where we now see the life we once knew as joyous memories knowing we had to face the blazing summers to get here. The winters where all the bad we see and had in our past can now be covered by the snow. To heal and hide the bad and only show the grace of forgiveness that covers it all. The lessons of life are shown to us in each moment of life, it is all in our search for what we are missing or needing that we can find it. I hope that you learn of the snow, find your strength, learn your solitude, embrace your journey downstream, understand that the angers and weakness only allow the greatness of life to continue on. Nature is a lesson and we are the students. The lessons it teaches us isn't only about life, but rather about ourselves as well. It is the understanding of man that causes the issues and it is the understanding of man that shows the natures as true. These are the lessons from above.

Pain

Pain, I feel so much pain. Waking up each day to the same fate. To rise hours before the sun, to drive countless hours back and forth to work. A job in which I despise. All that comes with who I am is neglected. I have a boss to please, orders to obey, times to be places, times to acknowledge my efforts. To drive countless hours more to return to my beginning dreams. Where chores need to be done, where fences constantly need fixed, where water is always scares, where barns never seem to stay standing, where shoes fall from horses, where saddles dry before oil can greet them again, and where spurs rust from the rode hard and put away wet mentality. Bills scalping my moments of trump. A house that is old beyond its years that needs to be mended and taken care of. To return hours after the sun goes down to sit behind technology that I also despise. To lay after all my strength has depleted from my body to drain my mind into pointless endeavors to sway a piece of paper above my head. Everything must be more important than the other in this life. Where all the time everyone pays me for is left standing in a rotting body of skin and bones. Where A brink is all that can allow an escape with a puff of smoke to ease my pain. The cars are in shambles, and the prices keep rising for all that live here relying on me. While my checks stay the same. Everyone still wanting more pieces of me to spend time with. I cannot allow my time to be wasted as I know I have so little. None of this is where the pain resides from though. The pain comes from knowing I ask God too much with little return to him. It comes from the distance between loved ones as my time must be only in glimpse to them, my dreams cannot come from scratch, and every divot I make seems to be washed away and pushed back further into my future. The pain comes from knowing those at my own home relying on me feel as though I need to change to be better and not knowing the demons from my past startle me in every waking moment of my improvement. Where are my joys? They are placed in the future which I cannot think about anymore, because they get annoying when it is all I can think about. I look forward to them only to let myself down knowing I have no time. Time eludes me and causes me stress. I relax between the hours of 11-3 an hour of waking up to begin again, no chances of weekend breaks as I fill them up with all I was too lazy to fulfill over the week. I constantly am in a rat race. Knowing I let God down from my actions of not having contentment, not resting in him, not building my future. Rather knowing I am in this rat race to try and produce something from nothing in man's world. Trying to appease everyone. If everyone only knew that my happiness would come if I was able to watch a sunrise and drink a pot of coffee as it come up on my front porch. To smoke without constant judgmental eyes glaring upon me, to have a few more beers because I am sore, and hurt. To Be allowed to ride my horse across pastures for pleasure instead of purpose. To dunk myself in the river when summer's get to me. To be able to speak my mind into truth where I am not compromised on a time, or a budget, but just allowed to speak so vicariously about my own freedom. To just take off to the places I have always wanted to see. Then to rest before the sun with a happy home of no fixings or chores left. Just to relax, to somber music and to wrap my arms in love with my family. I work so hard for that one day. I only let myself down as I hit the alarm clock again the next morning knowing I must put on a fake face of joy, to work harder than everyone else, to watch my body become ill of my schedule, to drive home to repeat a catering service of holding up my share of troubles. To then waste my mind away on things that mean nothing besides a piece of paper I have no intentions of having. To not relax for a minute, to not grab another beer, to quit smoking, and to stay up late again trying to push through my laziness. I let all those down in every way each day. That is where my pain comes from, and that is where it will call home in my heart until I finally snap one day, and pray that all I have done holds a strong enough bond to see me through. To be without pain would be strange to a man like me. So tomorrow please take it easy on me, I have many more of you to conquer before I can hold no pain.

The Land & Him

Resting in the hay loft. Sitting perched above the broken dust we call farm land. The views of spectacular pictures in every direction swallow up all the distilled air left from the march in. The sky places pieces of itself anywhere it can. As the profound array of red color wheel strikes the earth. It throws rhinestones over the cattle tank, as a soft breeze allows it to dance. Parading youth following mothers of every species fill the echoing noises found in the silence of evening. Trees that have outlived cultures stand dying amongst the thriving grounds. So baren with fractures of yesterdays. The feather of owls who call this loft home floats by me in a cascading ballet as it falls to the floor. Quiet scratching of wood grains whispers as mice tunnel in for the night. The screeching yells of cranes who enunciate their monkey howls to deaden the rustling as the sun sets. Looking over land more life, blood, and sweat has touched than many others will ever know. Oh the stories it could share of the arrowheads found in its soil, the carvings in boulders where wheat became dust, where bent trees marked the way across a desolate land, where fences grew old and died and were replaced by further generations. The stories of once holding blossoming love in the middle of nowhere. Now lies a couple miles from town. Where from the beginning of a home once thundered with hooves of bison, and equine. Still kept as thundering hooves from cattle, and horses strike the earth and leave their mark. Fires have scorched her, floods have drowned her, droughts have drained her, and worst of all man has used her. This tiny hamlet of nature is not unscathed, but still strong as buildings grow closer to her each day. Kept only by a note that has been late more times than not. This ground holds a job of paying for herself, only by the hands that work her. A kid who lost himself sits upon the barn left generations before to be the only legislator of her story. A peace keeper of tradition in time marks her different from all others. She has seen him bleed as the fences went up to protect her. She has watched him drenched in sweat as he moved the cattle who grazed her to a new home. She has watched him cry, as all he ever loved was lost to a piece of paper known only powerful to man. She has watched his head fall to the dirt as new colts needed guidance. She has cradled him when he marched her looking for food in winter. She has watched his eyes fill with love and passion as he masquerades around her. She has watched him love, and has blessed him with smiles. She knows he is only a glimpse in her life. She is thankful to still be her. Not to be changed even as she is used to protect herself. She knows the changing times have cut her water off from up stream. She knows the grasses that once so full now left bald as the creatures are trapped by the fences that outline her. She knows the blood rust roofs that have been all over her have fallen. She weeps as the young man who sits upon the barn overlooking her, will grow old before his time, and the miles he has trekked over her will weather his body. She knows he gives his life to her and all that it entails. So she does not mind the use of herself as she knows the young man contributes the same. She knows he crumbles knowing her future, and she does the same as she knows it is a life spent in vain keeping her alive. Aches from both man and land echo through the vibrance of life that are corralling here. The view from the loft window shows the work that has been done, and the work soon to be done. Hoping only for one more generation to fight as hard for the land to keep it the way it is. Life is only given because of the land, and all that humanity does is trying to escape from her. Only clinging to her when they themselves need something. The land will never die even as mankind does. She will survive to tell a thousand more lifetimes of stories. If only she could tell what she has already seen, to be convicted of the respect she deserves. All this lays in the blue eyes of a young man, out of breath from hay torn from the land, sweating as the temperature curses his body, tired from the forty hour work week he turned in before Tuesday, and the seventy more hours that sit and wait for him. The tattered cloth that he claims as clothes dangle from his carcass like moss. The hope the land sees in the young man's aspirations is worth the time it takes to tell their story. For the beauty he finds on her, to the new life he brings each fall, the guidance of adolescent colts, the scars of torn fence, the boots that line each post from the miles they drug through, the tire tracts of flowing through the land to allow her natural way to continue, and the view of home still stretched miles from the city. The skis will dim as they do on every day and on every story. The suns of yesterday's past still fill the night skies along the milky way tell him and her that there is a tomorrow, and the stories are never forgotten.

Endless Summer

$\mathcal{I}$f only there were a place of an endless early summer. Where the trees are so ambiguities with budding life. Where the wheat comes to an end with its fate as it begins to grow gold. Where birds never vanished from the bright colors of the skies. Where the sun rose early, and laid down late. Where clothes warm you in comfort in the morning brisk, and beg to be taken off by lights end. Where waters from spring stay plentiful on the prairies. Where music from all the generations can be heard driving through town with windows down. Where doors and windows to homes are opened welcoming the breeze of comfort that allows the curtains to sway in effortless dances. Where work in the elements seems to be a pleasure. Where the first strong storm approaches and the smell of thick rain clouds the nostrils and sparks love in a man's heart. Where suppers can be smelled halfway across the property. Where adolescent youths come out to venture on their own. Young fawns that wonder further each day from their mothers, where birds take their first flights. Where squirrels learn to trust in the next leap it takes. Chores seem like a blessing as they welcome another break for the animals best schedules. Whereas night falls the music of chattering owls barks from the woods like a Beethoven sonata lays in the valleys. The moon seems to act as a lamp leaving night only a slightly dimmer version than day. Where the milky way seems to race the sky as if a highway in Dallas. Crackling fires make for churches all summer. Where late night conversations are held of love, of memories, or tragedies, or hopes, of dreams, and of truths.

The first time a young man gets his father's truck to pick up his date and to treat her right. The memories of an endless summer would never get old. It would be only a wish. For without the seasonal change we could not appreciate the summers as we do. So for now we will wait for the blistering sun, we will pack our fires away, we will watch as rain collects in the bottoms, and we will peer out our widow and watch the moon lay upon the fences as if that's where it was made to be. We will hope for and endless summer, but be thankful when it is over. To dream of an endless summer is nice. The reality of it is what we crave. Catching that first fish of the year, and trying your best not to brag, the first tip toes stretched out into the lake testing the chances of being submerged. Cutoffs showing the towns peoples ink, and the styles the kids are setting trying to start a trend. The squeak of windmills that lay upon the land as tombstones of times forgotten where they stood for preservation. Oil rigs squeak as their worn out hydraulic jacks get low. The pressures released through the lines of a tractor. The dust that rolls up from the floorboards as you take the gravel road. Stored hay allowing the cattle to adventure along the freshly matured meadows, and the quiet neighs of horses feeling their oats. The tornados that swirl in the round corrals as colts begin to learn their fates. The thirst quenched after a long day seems less grim than those of winter. A time of peace as every time is a good time to be outside working on something. A time where hammocks sway and children play. An endless summer seems great to me. It comes sooner and sooner each year. For early summer does not last long, but rather it is just a glimpse of hope for that to come. For me the early summer is a place of greatness. The time where you think you can see it all coming together. The place where you can catch subtle breaks and see ugliness in natures. Where everything is thriving, pleasures are beginning to rise. Responsibilities are being let go for a moment. Early summer is a place I wish to live, if only for a while. It makes the year almost worth it. The early summer is a time of life, hope, escape, and dreams form. It is where you can stand to see the rest of the year. Knowing where the next will begin. When it begins to warm and water disappears I know it is gone, but I am always thankful for the memories I had in the short month of early summer. For it gives me joy to hold onto for the residing year ahead. An endless early summer is where my dream begins, and where I hope it ends. The thriving part of life, where all is enjoyed by everyone. Early summer please grace me with your presence. I have waited so long.

Busting Bronc Ballet

The morning crests the deceased souls that lay hollowed eyed. The blood flow for clambering metal slapping the fences. Long before domestication, this horse lay free among the public grounds. Trapped, scared, and trailered, this horse fought every step of the way. It stands alone in a glimpse of freedom, as the boundaries portrayed by the barbs that shimmer in the moonlight. Covering every inch of land in the first thirty minutes of his arrival now stands motionless. Freedoms were slowly gained on this new frontier. By the hands of a new master. Ropes burned the flesh, and erased the hairs on his neck. Now his feet weigh heavy as metal that is nailed into him. The split ears, streak faced, bow legged, pigeon toed, bronc that now wears the brand of a man. Each day much like the rest the chasing begins. The sun, not yet over the horizon as gates slam behind him. Ropes thrown over his head, and saddles swaying his back. Each day this horse fights at every hitch in the road, untrustworthy it seems. Those who try to tame the bronc lay sporadically down each night. One however, never gave in after being defeated time and time again. Until one day this bronc decided to defy the odds. Allowing the rider to take his back. Something learned that day for the both of them as they battled having a master. The horse looked to the man and the man looked to Christ. Both learning that the other was not there to break their spirit or tame their freedoms. Rather there only to guide. Never knowing their true purpose unless they trust their masters. Fighting for all of life to be free, and never knowing truly what freedom was without guidance to the right area. The man much like the bronc free among the youth of petulance. Tamed by the bills that trapped him on his land. Left to fight man until he decided one day to trust the rider of his soul. They rode out among the prairie blossoms and watched the life that happens each day pass before them. Days spent in the saddle turned to stories. Brandings turned to friendship, and competitions turned to glory. The Bronc & the Brute. As the dust settled on the career of them both the memories of the times spent getting thrown to the ground, the tragedies they faced together, the triumphs they won, and the life they shared growing more than they ever could. The rider's job is only to guide, to derive purpose, the job of horse is to trust, and to provide the work that comes with the opportunities given. In the end the bronc ballet is the battle of life.

Drive through Time

His knuckles white, his eyes glazed, his head is buzzed, his body aches, and his joys are outrunning the white lines. The songs that guide his thoughts based on his feelings keep him alive. Knowing there is something inside is better than knowing you can't feel a thing. He chooses pain over pride every day knowing that if he can feel physical pain it out runs the pain he feels inside every day he opens his eyes. Percocet only relaxes him anymore, not having the everlasting numbness they had before. The booze becomes more and more as his time gets shorter and shorter. It is a battle of monsters behind these leathered eyes. To give into a society he despises, to give into a woman who would never try to understand, to give into his pain and emotion, and to give up on the only thing he loves. This drive clears his mind each day as he counts the white lines. The only spotlight in his life that is a clear path is paved going to the next town. Nothing between them but thoughts and telephone wires. It is a part of heaven granted to the modern day. Old school doesn't describe him, he is out of time itself finding no reasoning with his joys stripped to continue on. Only knowing there is sin on the way out and he cannot condemn himself to that. It is the drive through time that gives him a break. A moment of isolation to cry, a moment of time where he can be alone with truly his own thoughts that are smarter than his actions. These moments where time doesn't exist is the only way for the man to survive. Tough love is still the only love he knows so he commits to the bad, because he saw what soft love could be in the beginning. Now his heart callused harder than his hands. The drive that separates time is the only time you can see a man cry alone, to smile alone, to think alone, and to pray alone. These moments wished they could be shared, but knowing the ridicule of the world and the home would judge him to the negative, making nothing better for the moment he is in. So, he keeps in more than he lets out, and lets it disappear and build as time slips away into music.

The Morning After

The morning after is the surreal moment of time where heaven's walkway aligns with the earth. Where the crass lay in perfect formations leaning forward stretching for the warmth they crave. Where rusted barbed wire drips from the frost leaving its decaying body. Birds pierce the silence of angels' choir with their own songs of life. Views that photos could never capture rapture the lives of those who crave the subtle blisses of oasis hidden among the common plains. Grooves that nestle the youth of repopulation from man. The crackling hedge branches slapping together as apples thunder upon the ground. The bickering barks of bushy tailed squirrels echo through the valley to the open sky. The baritone frogs creek out their morning voices to each other. The ear blistering noise of air being cut as divers float in from the clouds to find rest on the pond. The screams of hawks float among the hill tops as they scour the land of opportunity. The shuffle of flat stones falling over each other cascading into the water's edge as deer seek replenishment before grazing the day away. The scrapping thieves holler down the darkness of the timber. As coons scrimmage for their nights plunder with each other. The white cotton that purges itself from the tan ocean of prairie as a cotton tail wiggles its nose at what bouquets the land has created that day from them. The moaning hinges of corral gates left to rot a century before. As the wires hum a cracking glacier's song as coyotes slink through them in search of fun. Sitting perched above the view of life itself watching that of heaven pour out over the land blessing the rustic naturalism of colors and life. For no reason other than just to be. Simply captured through two eyes that have seen the sins serendipitous discoveries of the lost. The morning after is the savior of grace, the hope of good, and the praise of nature. The morning is where nothing has happened yet to set forth the ruthlessness of destruction. The morning is a new beginning filled with the glory of a new beginning. Determining where the day goes does not belong to nature. Yet, nature graces the day of its destruction by contributing to all that depends upon her. Skies stretch from horizon to horizon, with beds of angels flying with it. An enterprise of flight interrupts the imagination of reality as planes carry others miles away from what lays here below. As the sky reaches down to earth with its fingertips combing the hill sides with blue, whipping the gates of eternity away. Taking the colors of morning and spreading them to others who seek their new beginnings. Allowing the morning to be gone in what seems a breath. Allowing the day to take hold, and the unscripted debut of glory, and sin to battle over those who place their names on the land. Detrimental to her, nature gives to those who seek a better life, the opportunity of the morning after each day. For each morning is a new chance to welcome and enjoy her, she will never leave even after our mornings have passed. Still she returns to those who sit and welcome the life given each day. To the trees that enriched her soul, to the grasses that hide the toughness of her rocky past, the waters that cleanse her, the animals that create the balance she needs, and the men that created her very own submissive toxic relationship. Love and hate is the same feeling, only walking a line as to which side you fall on. Determines the effects that come from it. Each sharing a life altering heart ache that can only be filled by the other. It is a commitment to each other, and those who walk the line are swayed to love from the morning after. Those who barter with the night learn to hate her. The sensation of life glimmers like a diamond in the morning sun, the depths of despair hides in the shadows. For where there is light, there is dark, complimenting each other, symbolic only through the structures of life that create the distinction between them. As the morning after reveals them, it also gives them beauty even through decay. As you are perched among these hills, welcome the warmth as it crawls along your skin when light pierces the sleeping creations of life, capture the efforts of those who embrace the morning's new beginning, and be ignorant to those who heckle from the shadows. The nights are long and dark, but the mornings after begins with life, and light. Be the morning after in this life to those who praise it.

In memory of "Billy Jo" Kind